MW01181978

WHO KNEW?

RITA IRWIN-DAVIDSON

A portion of the proceeds from the
sale of this book will go to the
National Exchange Club's Foundation
for the Prevention of Child Abuse.

Acknowledgements

I want to acknowledge all the people who encouraged me to write this book and those who contributed to it.

My deep love goes to my compassionate husband, Rob Davidson, who cared for me and boosted my spirits every day during my bout with cancer—the surgery and the chemotherapy.

A thank you to my special friends Christina Duncan, Dian Howe, and Linda Seligman who constantly cheered me on to write a book.

A special thanks to my National Exchange Club friends who encouraged me in my recovery and urged me to publish my writing.

I want to thank my husband, Rob Davidson, MBA, Jane Meyers, Ph.D. in Curriculum Studies, and Michael Ames, for editing this book.

I want to acknowledge artists Jennifer Basurto, Nick Castor, and Mosade Virgil from the TUSD Museum for the Visual Arts for their illustrations.

This book is dedicated to Maureen Schertzer, Veronica Blake, Nancy Bowland, and Mary Helen High. Without my asking them, these very special women stayed with me each night in the hospital as I recovered from my surgery.

I also want to thank Margaret Hoeft, Elizabeth Jackson, Beth Ann Johnson, Cheryl Lawson, Linda Leighton, Kathy Locke, Sue Peterson, Char Soliday and neighbors, Cynthia and Stuart Garrison for their kindness.

I want to thank my friends Sherry Felix and Renetta Larson for their kindness and support.

If I have forgotten anyone, please blame it on "chemo brain."

Rita Irwin-Davidson

To order more books contact Rita at ritapriscilla@aol.com.
The cost per book is $10.00 with $2.00 going to the National
Exchange Club Foundation for the Prevention of Child Abuse.

Chapter 1

A thank you to Sam and Ethel, my grandparents

By crossing a great ocean and stepping onto Ellis Island, my grandparents saved me from a life of hard labor in Siberia or an agonizing death in the gas chambers of Nazi Germany. Does being an American mean anything to me? It means my life.

My grandparents individually left Poland and Russia to go see the "land of milk and honey." A land they had heard was paved with streets of golden opportunity for all people, regardless of religion or race. They met an America of 1906, teeming with immigrants like themselves. My grandmother worked fourteen hours a day as a seamstress in a sweatshop on New York's Lower East Side. My grandfather sawed lumber and built cabinets for the B. and O. Railroad.

Both moved to Indianapolis, where they met and married. They opened a corner market and produced four children. My mother, Fay, was the oldest. "Education is the way to get ahead in this country," they told their children. "No one can take an education away from you." However, the Great Depression of the 1930s quashed any hopes of college. The children, now young adults, helped in the business so the family could survive.

World War II emerged from the ashes of Pearl Harbor. One son went off to war to fight for his parents' adopted country. The rest of the family collected scrap metal and bore the burden of rationed meat and gasoline along with other Americans.

The war ended and my grandfather's health began to fail. The doctor warned that if he didn't leave Indianapolis' chilling winters he would die within six months. My grandparents sold everything and packed up the family for a 2500 mile move to Tucson, Arizona. The dry, desert heat helped my grandfather live thirteen more years. He was gentle and kind to everyone. He would let me follow him along on all his errands during those adolescent summers that seemed so endless. He died a few months after he and my grandmother had celebrated their fiftieth anniversary. My grandmother lived the last ten years of her life with us, but she was never the same.

I wish I could thank my grandparents now for giving me the gift of freedom. They understood what the United States meant—a land of diverse people trying, not always succeeding, but constantly striving to preserve and expand an individual's, a family's, a group's, and a nation's right to be free.

Chapter 2

I Can't Take It!

I can't take this anymore! The frustration; the kids' lack of respect; the parents' attitudes; the paperwork; the loss of support for a profession in which I've invested thirty years of my life.

I'll quit. I'll withdraw my retirement and start my own business. Every year for at least the last five years of my teaching, I've gone through this dilemma. Convincing myself that I've definitely paid my dues to society by educating tomorrow's future. I start out each summer to embark upon a new career. Yet, every time the school bell rings, I find myself back in a classroom ready to nudge, poke, prod and inspire my students into appreciating the joys of the English language.

Why would a person subject herself to this nine and half month torture every year? Money? Fame? I think not. I know not.

Lest one think I'm out of my mind, perhaps a few examples would be in order for an understanding of this masochistic behavior.

William Shakespeare's play "Macbeth" is a requirement for most students to read in their sophomore year. We study Shakespeare's life as well as the play. This year I tried some new techniques for teaching "Macbeth"—from having the students act out battles to showing a rather gory but finely acted and updated version of the Shakespearean classic. I was really looking forward to reading the students' reactions to the unit.

I sat down with the tests and began to read:

"I don't really remember much of Bill Shakespeare's life, but I can tell you that he is one of my favorite writers of all time."

"Macbeth was told not to fear anyone born of woman, so that is why Macduff was able to kill Macbeth, because Macduff was born seasection."

Perhaps more personal examples will illustrate my lemmings' trip to the sea each school year.

While I was teaching in junior high some years back, there was a student I'll call Cal. He was a teacher's nightmare—restless, hyper, and always ready for a fight. He came to school dressed in hand-me-downs. His face was usually smudged with grease and his arms were often bruised.

I asked the school counselor about Cal's background. She investigated and reported that Cal lived with his mother and older brother. His mother was an alcoholic who was rarely home, and his brother and Cal regularly got into fights.

One of Cal's special "attention getters" was to ask to be excused to use the restroom. Upon returning, he'd stop outside my room, squat down, and walk his fingers up the window, monster-style. The class would burst out giggling while I was in the midst of explaining some life-altering bit of grammar. Cal was a joy.

That summer I managed to persuade his mother to let Cal travel to Disneyland with me. It was his first visit. He was thirteen years old. Just watching his eyes light up as we toured the park made it the best visit to Disneyland I had ever experienced.

Along with the Cals come the Annes. Anne was so serious. She rarely smiled, but her eyes said, "I am willing to learn."

Then, for over a week, Anne didn't come to class. I was concerned and called her home. It seems her brother had committed suicide the previous weekend. When Anne returned to school, we talked. Of all her brothers and sisters she had been the closest to her brother, so she blamed herself for not being able to reach him. What I did for Anne was listen. Later in the year, at her request, we attended a Doobie Brothers concert together. My hearing has never been the same. Yet I wouldn't trade that concert with Anne for an evening with James Michener.

So here's to "Bill" Shakespeare and all the Cals and Annes in my future classes. I raise my glass of wine, of which I will probably need many until my retirement, and I salute you.

You are my reason for teaching.

Sports CAR 2

Chapter 3

The Red Sports Car

Since I turned forty, the quest for great sex and the search for the meaning of life have been uppermost in my thoughts. These dilemmas plus making sure the house is neat and clean—a fragmentary lapse to a bad habit—have obsessed me of late. I mull over the two enigmas while peeling the outer leaves off a head of lettuce. The water from the tap runs into the cored-out center; then, like magic, the leaves of the lettuce come off and are washed clean. This technique, one that has won me no career opportunities nor male admirers, was instilled in me, and many other unsuspecting young females, in my junior high home ec class by Mrs. Dora Bunch, she of the infamous black beehive hairdo and white sauce. I really shouldn't make fun of this lettuce washing process, since turning forty and eating more salads seem synonymous. I now consume large quantities of salads in an effort to stem the rising tide of my soaring abdomen. Where did this enlarged midriff come from? I have to exercise my rear end off just to look plump.

Exercise videos have become my salvation. I've noticed these have been toned down from the initial ones that came out. The first ones to appear seemed geared toward those people training for a Mt. Everest climb. Now they have been modified and made more practical, one of the latest being a routine for people who get out-of-breath just putting clothes in a washer.

But this deviates from my premise of how turning forty has led to my search for great sex and the meaning of life. One thing I've discovered is that "great sex" is different for each person. Another noteworthy, but not startling, discovery is that it almost always exists at the beginning of relationships and seems to ebb as the years flow by. The former also holds true for the meaning of life. But, as one turns forty, great sex and the meaning of life seem to take on more importance. Perhaps it's a sense of time running out. However, I have managed to overcome the forty hump with one single purchase—a bright, red, turbo-engine sports car. I suggest you try it. Your life will change dramatically. Admiring stares will greet you at stop lights. Strange men will approach you in parking lots (make sure you have your can of Mace handy). These men will range in age from twenty to seventy. They will be all shapes and from all professions and ethnic groups. They will comment first on how great your car looks. Then they will inquire about its handling performance and ask how fast it will go.

Something seems to happen to a man's psyche when he views a woman in a red sports car. His heart beats faster and his imagination runs to the wild side. I've even had very conservative-looking men in their pin-striped suits tell me that they drive a BMW or Volvo for that image of career stability, but they'd really like to drive a flashy, red sports car.

Last week I went for my yearly eye exam. The thirty–something, handsome ophthalmologist smiled at me and asked if that was my little red sports car parked out in front? I said it was, and he went on to ask the usual questions I get about speed and performance. "Those cars look like a lot of fun!" he said with a grin. I'd won his admiration, and, before I'd left his office, an invitation to dinner.

So, if turning forty is going to be traumatic, and if there recently have been a shortage of men in your life, it's not too late. Buy yourself a bright, red sports car. If you feel this suggestion is too superficial, then I'm truly sorry if I've offended you. Because if, after forty, you still believe that lasting relationships are based on similar values, things in common, and passionate love-making, then you need to get yourself a van.

Chapter 4

Holiday Flu Blues

Being home sick with the flu is the pits. But, at holiday time, it's even worse. While other people are out doing their Christmas shopping and partying, I'm stuck in the house, lying in bed feeling miserable.

"Well," I say to myself, "if I have to stay home for awhile, I might as well make the best of it."

So I gather together the newspaper, all those old magazines I haven't had a chance to read for a month, and the T.V. Guide. The newspaper lifts my spirits with articles on world economic collapse and a story on a guy who took his twenty-two and shot twelve holes into his T.V. set because he was upset with the weather forecast.

Next, I pick up a magazine. This particular magazine specializes in articles on how to start your own business. The first article relates how this person made $50,000 his first five months in business with no investment and no risk. Another article tries to convince me to work from home by doing really intellectually stimulating work like stuffing envelopes. Then there is an ad informing me that I can "Earn up to $25.00 an hour repairing vinyl." I jot down the phone number listed on the ad as a possible career after I retire.

Browsing through another magazine, I find an article that makes me feel guilty about my efficiency on the job. "We'll show you how to work sixty times faster" it blares. As if I wanted to. I got sick because I was so stressed out from overwork that my body picked up the first disease to come along. Luckily, it was only the flu.

Then I begin perusing one of the traditional women's magazines which still haven't discovered that most of us women are working outside the home, so they come up with projects for us like "Redo Your Kids Furniture" or "How to Host a Crowd." I suppose my kids' furniture could use some redoing, although I've really become attached to the orange crates and blocks. As far as hosting a crowd, in our house everyone has to fend for themselves when it comes to a meal—if they want to eat.

Finally, I pick up a new kind of women's magazine. It gives me tips on the "Secrets of Sensational Sex." Since the flu has left me feeling demolished and looking like Phyllis Diller—pre-five face lifts. I'll keep these tips for later reference.

In a desperate attempt to alleviate my ennui, I turn to the T.V. Guide. The most exciting programs on right now are "Gynecology Update" and "Living With Diabetes."

Just as my boredom reaches its peak, our German shepherd, Mattie, hops up on the bed with her favorite chartreuse tennis ball in her mouth, as if to say, "Why don't you do something productive like throwing my ball for me?" For several hours, Mattie has been terrorizing our Siamese cat, Doris, by chasing her around the house. Doris finally decided "enough of this" and has retreated into an upstairs closet for some afternoon meditation. After a few minutes of ball throwing for Mattie, which entails (no pun intended) wrestling the ball from her formidable jaws, I find myself weary and settle back for a short nap. In a few hours, "It's a Wonderful Life" will be on, and tomorrow I may have the energy to begin that new Danielle Steel novel I've been wanting to read. Maybe I'll even tackle our Christmas card list and get them out to our friends before New Year's as I did last year.

Chapter 5

Our First Cat—Doris

Closet doors ajar, window blinds halfway up, and small paw prints across a glass table—all tell-tale signs of a house with a cat—our house. But, our house wasn't always like this.

It began a few months ago when I saw my neighbor out walking his poodle. A small Siamese-looking cat followed behind them. I commented on what a lovely and friendly cat this creature seemed to be.

"Oh, yeah, she's friendly. Ya know somebody who might want her?" asked the neighbor. "She's a stray. I've been feeding her but I can't let her into my house. I already have two cats, a dog, and a gerbil."

Being of sound mind and soft heart, I said that I would ask around and see if I could find some sucker—I mean caring person—to take the cat. After calling several friends and getting refusals, I mulled it over in my mind. I'd never owned a cat, and our dog, Mattie, needed some company because my husband and I weren't home a lot. So, I found the sucker to take the cat—me.

We named her Doris. There was no logic involved, just gut reaction. We thought about an elegant Oriental name, since the cat looked Siamese, but we didn't want to offend our dog, Mattie, with a cat in the house named after possible royal lineage.

As Doris wandered around our house for the first time, I realized why I had wanted her so badly. She was a gorgeous cat. Her pale blue eyes peered out from a beige and chocolate-colored face. Her body also was beige, with her ears and tail picking up the chocolate coloring on her face. She was small—possibly ten pounds tops—and she was soft and warm.

After fifteen minutes of observing Doris explore our house, I put Mattie in the yard and drove off to the nearest mega-pet store. I charged around the store with a sense of elation—purchasing first a custom-designed litter box with a three-month charcoal filter, then a new type of kitty litter that can be scooped up and flushed directly into the toilet. What a great idea! (I learned later, after Roto Rooter left our house, not such a great idea) Next I picked up ten cans of gourmet cat food, three catnip toys; a mauve-colored carpeted scratching post, and tuna-flavored kitty treats.

As I checked out, I exclaimed to the cashier that this was my very first cat! She looked up at me and smiled weakly as if to say, "That's great, lady, but I'm busy, and I see people like you every day. So, chill out!"

I raced home to present Doris with all the wonderful goodies I'd purchased, but Doris wasn't impressed. She preferred scratching the moldings around our doors to her mauve-colored, carpeted scratching post. And, instead of playing with any of her expensive toys, she chewed on our clock radio antenna and batted around the mini-blind pullers.

This obsession of Doris' with tearing up the moldings has caused us much consternation. I've called just about every pet outlet in town. It seems carpeted scratching posts are "in" this season and the wooden ones, preferred by Doris, are "out". Adding to this dilemma, my husband has volunteered to construct a wooden scratching post. "How hard can it be?" he says. "I guess not as hard as the time you tried to shave a few inches off the bottoms of our doors so the new carpeting would fit," I retorted. He rolls his eyes at me. Our doors are a bit wavy at the bottoms now, but you can't tell how uneven they are unless you lie belly-down on the carpeting and peer under each door. Luckily, not too many of our guests have done that.

We've had Doris for almost six months now. Every day I find out something new about her. She loves the darkness of closets yet still enjoys basking in the sun on a window sill. She moves about the house with grace and elegance, and takes life so calmly. I think we will learn a lot from her.

Meow

Jennifer Basuelo

18

Chapter 6

There is no cat like Mousie.

He was completely grayish silver. He had one green eye and one hazel eye. As cats go, Mousie was not the handsomest guy in town. But oh, how he made up for it in personality. His appetite for food was as voracious as his affection for people. He devoured chicken, ham, beef, and was especially fond of shrimp. But, most of all, he relished people. He would sit on anyone's lap. The minute I would lie down, he was there to snuggle up "on" me. I say "on" me because that's exactly where he was. He placed his body on my chest with his head in the crux of my armpit and his paws stretched over my arm. The closer he came to me the more comfortable he would become. He enjoyed having the top of his head kissed and caressed and his neck and tummy were fair game for petting profusely. In fact, Mousie was just one "purring love machine." If I had a task to perform that required only one hand, I scooped up Mousie with my other hand, placed him on my arm and carried him around the house while I worked. He liked to be part of what was going on. Being cradled in my arms like a baby and transported about was heaven to Mousie.

But all good things must come to an end. So, last week because Mousie no longer cared for his favorite foods, because he cried out in pain at night, because he was getting so thin and weak, but mainly because I could not stand to see him suffer, I took him to the vet and comforted him while he was administered his fatal shot. Mousie was twenty years old. He lived a long, full, loving life, but I would greedily have wanted him to live twenty more.

A few days after I had to have Mousie "put down," I opened my appointment book to the following week. There, stuck to the page, was a piece of Mousie's fur—a small, gray shred telling me, "Don't forget me too quickly, now." Don't worry, Mousie, I will never forget you. You will always be a part of me. There is no cat like Mousie.

Chapter 7

Troubling Technology

Technology has hit our home big time! We have satellite television—which, for my husband Rob, is a bit of heaven on earth. He can now remotely flip through not just forty, but two hundred channels of electronic drivel. He gets football games year-round and horse racing from tracks across the U.S. He can watch five different episodes of Star Trek on five different channels simultaneously, flicking from one station to another.

Since we've gotten satellite television, I've read several good books and have begun redecorating the house. Operating the satellite system is still a mystery to me. It seems our house wasn't wired properly for the "Great Satellite in the Sky," meaning you need an I.Q. of 180 just to figure out how to switch it on. Also, due to the wiring screw-up, turning on each T.V. in the house must be done in a different way. Rob reads off the instructions for each one as I carefully jot them down. There are five steps to just turning on the living room T.V., three steps for turning on the back bedroom T.V., but only two steps for turning on the master bedroom T.V. This causes me much aggravation as it took me an eon to get used to the cable system and two more eons to learn how to record a tape on our VCR. (I am not a moron, just technologically challenged.)

As if my life isn't complicated enough, it seems the local channels now have new numbers for the satellite T.V. This cuts to the core of my very being: my cultural upbringing. After watching these channels for over forty years, their numbers ingrained in my subconscious, now they are no longer the familiar channels of my youth. Channel 13 is now 412. Channel 4 is now 5316, and channel 9 is an infinite number. This drastic change in local channel numbers causes me to yearn for the "good old days" of no channel number above fifteen.

Because our house is so unique for satellite use, the efficiency of the satellite performance has come into question several times.

Of course, this is only in my mind. My husband says operating the system is "a piece of cake." This makes me feel more technologically inadequate, as it takes me half an hour just to turn on the T.V. in the living room. One night, I was watching a movie on our number one bedroom T.V. set. The picture became blurry with streaks of snow, so I called my husband, who was watching the living room T.V., and asked him if he had any disturbance in his picture. He came into the bedroom and said, "No." Then he nonchalantly added that our neighbor was probably using her microwave.

"You mean every time our neighbor uses her microwave, we'll get interference on our T.V?" I asked in amazement.

"Only on the bedroom T.V.," my husband calmly replied, and went back to his watching of the living room T.V. which apparently is not affected by our neighbor's microwave.

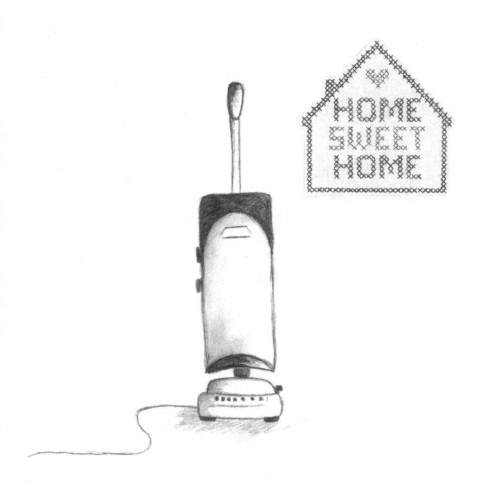

Chapter 8

Vacuum Cleaner I

Greetings and Happy New Year to all our family and friends:

This year found me supporting the economy with frequent visits to Ross's, Walmart, Steinmart, Target, and short stints in Nordstrom's and IKEA. Now, my patriotism cannot be questioned; however, Rob feels I need to express my love for our country in ways other than spending us into bankruptcy.

Gort, our English bulldog, is an unending source of income for our vet. Since the doctor doesn't have any children to put through college, I assume we've paid for a few fancy vacations by now for him and his wife. Gort is allergic to "something" as yet undetermined. He is constantly afflicted with skin lesions on his belly and lower extremities. For this he needs antibiotics which we obtain by prescription from Walgreens. Gort Davidson is now a celebrity name at our neighborhood Walgreens. Actually, Gort was not his name when we got him. It was "Dollar"—a premonition of what was to come. Gort now sleeps at the foot of our bed. This means it's imperative that I go to sleep before Rob and Gort doze off or I will have to drift into slumberland between the sounds of a jack-hammer and a chainsaw.

Ginger, our nine-year-old cat, is constantly being chased around the house by Gort. Ginger is a "lady" and doesn't wish to associate with a vulgar, smelly, drooling, stinky, gas-producing, food-driven animal. She believes in rest and lots of it, naps that last about twelve hours, leisurely eating, self-grooming her fur to a luster. She enjoys neck rubs and a frolic in warm clothes just removed from the dryer. One hobby of hers is to swat pens and stray change off any flat surface. I'm sure that behind most of our bureaus and bookcases lies a fortune in coins.

But enough "fluff." Now for the real problems in our world: forget the war in Iraq, terrorism, and torture. Here are some of the struggles we've battled this past year: the fracas with the vacuum cleaner; the disputed territory of the recycled goods, and the havoc with the vibrating toothbrush.

Vacuum cleaners frequently seem to come and go in our house. They start off like new relationships—all smooth and stable...then the weird sounds start—a grind here—a clunking there. Call me paranoid, but I know the makers of vacuum cleaner bags have it in for me! The bag's hole never seems to fit the vacuum's hole. By the time I clip the bag into the vacuum, I've worked up a sweat and used language that my parents taught me never to say. Now I'm in no mood to vacuum. I wasn't in the mood to begin with. Finally, I plug it in and turn on the switch. The smell of dirty rags spews into the room. I open it up and throw in a sheet of Bounce. After vacuuming the entire house, my lower back is killing me because most vacuums are made for midgets (oops! I mean "little people"). Today, my vacuum wasn't picking up even the largest piece of lint, so I dragged it into Smith's Vacuum and Sewing to be serviced. I had thoughts of abandoning it there. When they call me to say it's ready, I'm going to say that the Davidsons have moved leaving no forwarding address.

I pride myself on my recycling. It is probably the only thing I do to help clean up the environment. However, it is amazing how my recycling has mushroomed. At Thanksgiving , my brother-in-law spilled some crumbs and wanted to vacuum them up. He opened the hall closet where the vacuum is stored. A barrage of egg cartons, tin foil, and plastic containers toppled onto him.

"What's all this garbage doing in your house?" he asked.

"That's not garbage!" I retorted. "It's recyclable goods."

"It looks like garbage to me."

Some people just don't appreciate altruistic efforts.

Browsing through Walgreens on one of my economic safaris, I discover a vibrating toothbrush for only five dollars. Not only does the stem of the toothbrush vibrate, but some of the bristles twirl and swirl. There is a tiny rubber bulge on the top of the handle that turns it on and a tiny rubber bulge on the bottom of the handle that turns it off. One morning, after brushing my teeth with this "technological wonder for the masses," I put it back into the ceramic toothbrush holder on the sink and left the bathroom. All hell broke loose. A terrible clanging reverberated through the house. I thought the water pipes were coming apart. I panicked as thoughts of thousands of dollars in plumbing fees raced through my brain. Then I remembered that I had forgotten to turn off the toothbrush. I rushed back into the bathroom where the toothbrush and its holder were vibrating their way to San Diego. With a sigh of relief, I pushed the lower button which turned off this scientific marvel.

So, as you can see, since my retirement I have had an exceedingly exciting life—much like those lives seen on soap operas or the Harry Potter flicks—a life filled with frustration, fulfillment, and danger. And, I wouldn't have it any other way.

HAVE A WONDERFUL YEAR!

Chapter 9

VACUUM CLEANER II

Dear Friends and Family: Happy Holidays!

I hope you all are enjoying the true spirit of the holiday season—one of love and caring. I end the year with a sigh of relief, knowing that I've tried to tackle the problems that are within my control.

Those keeping up with the vacuum cleaner saga will remember how difficult it was for me to get the bag to stay in the hole. Well, one day the vacuum cleaner, whose brand shall remain nameless (this letter may get into the hands of a lawyer, and I don't want to get sued for libel), stopped picking up lint and started making a grinding noise. I tried to tune it out but the carpeting wasn't looking too great even after vacuuming. So, I took it into Smith's, our local multi-million dollar company that services vacuum cleaners. The customer rep said the belt had broken. The vacuum was full of goop. I left it there hoping never to see it again. Unfortunately, they told me to call on Thursday to see if it was ready. On Thursday, I called. They couldn't find it. My heart jumped with joy. Time and time again they put our phone number into the computer. The name Davidson did not come up. Visions of a bag-less vacuum cleaner danced in my head. Then they said that the name Irwin was the only one under that number. Now I could have denied that my maiden name was Irwin, but I wasn't quick enough. "Oh, that's me," I said. With a heavy heart that day I went to pick up the freaking vacuum cleaner. It's baaaack! to give me more hours of aggravation and irritation. I've got a plan. I'm going to tell Rob that Smith's said that it's unfixable, donate it to Good Will and treat myself to a "bag-less" vacuum cleaner for Hanukkah. Luckily Hanukkah comes early this year. "Hasta la vista, baby."

Speaking of picking up dirt, my mouth seems to be an expert at picking up animal hair. Anyone who has ever lived with animals, especially cats, knows how cat hair with its light texture can float around a house and land anywhere. Our cat, Gingie, must shed at least a pound of cat hair yearly. She likes to sit on my lap in the morning while I drink my coffee and read the morning paper. Sometimes, of course, she sits on the paper, which makes it difficult to read. Why do cats like to do this? I want to hire a pet psychologist to delve into Gingie's "pea-size" brain and find out the reason she likes newsprint for her tushie. Anyway, as I read, Gingie wants me to pet her. I do pet her periodically between sips of coffee. The other day I started coughing and coughing. Something was coming up from my throat. I spit up a hairball! (only kidding). But I hasten to say that I'm sure if I ever have my gallbladder removed, the med tech doing the biopsy will be sifting through a gallbladder filled with gobs of cat hair.

I hate to drop names, however, this is a holiday letter—sometimes better known as "bragging mania," but before the recent November election, we had calls from Rudy Guiliani, Senator John McCain, former President Bill Clinton, AND, AND, the President of the United States, George Bush. Well! You can imagine our level of self-importance went sky high. To think these important men would call to ask for OUR vote! Don't envy us. We can't help it if we're on the "A" list.

By the way, if your holiday shopping and decorating becomes too hectic, I've got a great idea for a "fun" break. Sit down for a few minutes, take a deep breath, and read through the movies in the TV guide in the Sunday paper. For a good laugh and a query to your brain of "What lunatic producers put up the money for this movie?" try paging through the description under the titles. I found some very profoundly thoughtful movies:

Wrong Turn, "Inbred cannibals terrorize six stranded motorists." Isn't it difficult to be an inbred cannibal? Perhaps they ate an ancestor or two. Don't ask intelligent questions, just move on to the next title which isn't a great advertisement for bed-and-breakfast establishments: *Dead and Breakfast,* "Zombies attack people barricaded in a bed-and-breakfast." And last, but not least, a company unveils a radical concept of memory resculpting. This movie is titled, "Brain Dead," which is what your brain will be if you watch the above-mentioned movies.

My final commentary may be too indelicate for a holiday letter but, of course, that never stopped me before. Since Rob and I have been doing a lot of traveling for the National Exchange Club, I've become a reluctant expert on women's public bathrooms in airports. The main aspect of these bathrooms that bothers me is the paper toilet covers which rarely stay on the toilet seat. First of all, they're made from the flimsiest paper— better used in holiday pageants as gossamer wings for angels. Trying to pry this paper cover out of the metal cover holder without ripping the paper to shreds is your first challenge. If it does make it out of the container, you next must punch out the middle part of the cover and place it on the toilet seat. How one does this so that the cover remains on the seat while you put your derrière down has always eluded me. The whoosh of the air from my swooping rear-end seems to carry the paper toilet seat cover off the toilet seat onto the floor as my buttocks set themselves down on the uncovered seat. If the paper does stay on the seat, the flushing of the self-flushing toilet grabs it and carries it down, down into the depths of the sewer. Some of these toilets seem to have gone berserk and have a life of their own, happily flushing every few seconds giving you the bidet effect whether you want it or not. The really ironic part of this whole saga is that if you do manage to get the cover to stay put, when you get up and the toilet flushes the toilet seat cover remains securely glued to the seat. Go figure!

HAVE A WONDERFUL CHRISTMAS, HANUKKAH, KWANZAA, AND ANY OTHER WINTER HOLIDAY YOU WANT TO CELEBRATE, AND A HAPPY, HEALTHY NEW YEAR.

Chapter 10

Daddy comes to live with us.

Two years ago our lives changed dramatically when I had to make the decision to put my mother into a nursing home. Then my ninety-one-year-old father came to live with us. I became the dreaded "child/parent." Our once couple-centered household now circled around the needs of a ninety-one year old dynamo. My father was ninety-one, but most people thought he was seventy. He was in great shape except for some hearing loss and arthritis in his hands. He smiled constantly and always found the good in everything. He no longer drove, had stopped at eighty-nine after crashing into an inconveniently placed light pole, so he needed transportation to his monthly union and community service meetings.

Every morning he had to have a white grapefruit—not ruby-red but white—grapefruit. If you've ever looked for white grapefruit, you'll soon discover they are as rare as Captain Ahab's Great White Whale. One day while searching for the white grapefruit, we ended up at Costco. Daddy was hungry and had to be fed. I got him a hotdog and a piece of pizza. As my father sat down at one of the tables, thinking the stool he was about to sit on had a back he leaned back and fell onto the cement floor, slightly bumping his head. Five people rushed over to us. One man yelled, "Don't move him! Don't touch him!" I smiled at the man, picked up my father, put him back on the stool, and said, "We don't interrupt my father while he's eating." With that my father sank his teeth into the cheese pizza and commenced his meal. Food was of utmost importance to my father—concussions and back injuries could wait.

Daddy didn't demand much, but he had to have every bill paid the minute the mailperson delivered it or a terrible tragedy would befall him. Why I don't know. Since my husband and I both worked outside our home, we didn't even have time or want to take time to look at our mail until Saturdays. We paid our bills regularly every two weeks. Our creditors had never objected, but my father saw this as being irresponsible.

My father did not like to be left at home if we went anywhere. He walked, albeit slowly, but without a walker or a cane. He was fiercely independent in this respect. So, if we were invited anywhere, Daddy went with us. He participated in Super Bowl parties and many of our friends' birthday parties. He frequently went to the movies with us and just as frequently fell asleep during the movie. Then he'd begin to snore. I'd nudge him a bit and he'd wake up, naturally wanting to know what happened while he was asleep. I was ready to scream!

My father also accompanied us on vacations. We'd take him to Las Vegas every Christmas. Immediately upon entering a casino, he'd walk up and down a few rows of slot machines, deem one of them "lucky," and plant himself there for the next five hours. One of us had to stay nearby in case he needed to use the bathroom, as we had to guard the machine from other players while he was gone. This included bringing him his lunch and dinner. If Daddy won a twenty-five dollar jackpot in five hours, he was elated. After many hours, my husband and I, exhausted, pleaded with my father to go upstairs and rest. If he'd won more than one jackpot, he considered himself on a roll, and we had to physically pry him away from the slot machine with the promise that he could return later in the day. Naturally, we had to jot down the number of the machine to make sure we could find it again.

Because of my father's age, when he had to go to the bathroom he had to go. I had a lot of curious looks from people as I loitered outside men's public restrooms waiting for my father.

Every week my father bought Fantasy, Lotto, and Powerball tickets. Every week he knew that if he had played the numbers he had the week before, he would have won. If he won the big jackpot, he planned on rescuing my mother from the nursing home.

My father loved to be waited on. My mother really spoiled him. My husband washed his own clothes and got his own dinner. He looked at me scurrying around my father with my teeth clenched and just shook his head. "He can do a lot of that himself," snorted my husband. "It's good exercise!" He was right. But, my father was almost ninety-four. He had worked hard for most of his life. He'd have given us anything that was in his power to give. So I got him his tea and made him his meals.

One summer we rented a condo in San Diego that was nine stories above the beach. We gazed out over the ocean waves, their peaks glistening from the light of the full moon. We turned on the T.V. to watch, but mostly to listen to, the Three Tenors Concert featuring Pavarotti, Domingo, and Carreras. My father relaxed into a comfortable chair taking in the magnificent scene and the glorious voices. He looked so at peace. "This is as good as it gets," he sighed. At that moment I forgot all the work my father had been for me over the last few years. I forgot how disjointed our life had become and I was glad that I had been able to have this precious time with my special daddy. "I think so, too," I said.

Chapter 11

We Get a Gift.

When my ninety-four year-old father died after living with us for three years, I was devastated. We had grown so close during his stay with us. He was ninety-four, but acted like seventy-four. Fiercely independent, he never used a walker or a cane.

Daddy was supposed to move with us into a house that we were having built. He had even helped us pick out the lot and floor plan but he died before the house was finished.

Our old home sold and closed in a month, so we had to look for a place to stay until our new home was completed. Having a fifty-pound German shepherd was an obstacle in renting a decent apartment, so we found a small townhouse that allowed larger pets.

Two months after we moved into the townhouse, on the night in April,1997, that the University of Arizona men's basketball team won the NCAA national championship, another miracle occurred. Amidst the upstairs and downstairs TVs blasting away the last few seconds of our overtime win, and the radio blaring the exciting commentary to Arizona fans whose horns were honking with the enthusiasm of an unbelievable win, I heard "Meow, meow." It was coming from the back porch. I listened again. "Meow! Meow!" It was definitely a commanding force calling me to open the sliding glass door. I did, and there below me was a multi-colored kitty who looked up at me with demanding green eyes. "Meow," she cried as if to say, "What took you so long!" Then she sashayed in and jumped up on the couch.

My husband, not a real cat lover, said she probably belonged to a neighbor. I said she was a gift in celebration of the Arizona Wildcats' win. My husband said we'd have to find the owner. "Okay, tomorrow I'll ask around the townhouse complex," I said, knowing, as the new arrival snuggled up to me on the couch, that my search for its owner would take about five minutes. This kitty wasn't sent to celebrate the team's win. She was sent to help me heal from my father's death. She was sent so that every day after work, when the grief would hit the hardest, I could look forward to coming home to this soft, loving, amusing kitten, who entertained me with her fascination with paper bags and shoelaces, and who lived to be unendingly caressed.

Today, two years later, we are in our new home with Ginger, no longer a kitten but a full-grown Tabby. She has no fear of our dog, in fact they regularly play together. She is still enthralled with paper bags and has added water to her repertoire of phenomena about which she is so curious.

Six weeks ago my mother died. Ginger is there for me again— purring and cuddling and racing through the house chasing a moth. She says, "Live life in the moment. Have fun. Enjoy each day. And, oh, don't forget to ask for and give lots of love. That's what it's all about, isn't it?"

Chapter 12

April, 1999

Yesterday

As the golden dusk of sunset covers the desert with the rosy glow of twilight, my mind wanders back twenty years.

My parents were living in their own home, retired and enjoying a life they had worked so hard to achieve.

It was the year after my divorce that, at the time, seemed the worst thing that had ever happened to me. Now, in retrospect, it was the best thing that ever happened to me. It gave me the opportunity to do, at thirty-one, what I should have been doing at twenty-one, living on my own and making my own decisions. My life now took the pathway to a new marriage with a wonderful man.

I never wanted to move far from my parents. My mother and father were very loving, understanding people. I was an only child, spoiled with attention and over-protected. My parents were at fault for this, but I let them do it. I knew if I got into trouble, financially or emotionally, they would always be there for me. Oh, how I took them for granted!

My wonderful, blue-eyed, life-loving father died three and half years ago. He was ninety-four. He woke up every morning with a smile, saying, "Top of the morning to ya." It took him three days to die. As he lay in the hospital bed, I cried and draped myself over him, murmuring into his ear how much I loved him and how I appreciated his always being there for me. He was too weak to speak but his eyes blinked to signal that he had heard me.

Two years later, as my mother lay dying, I climbed into bed with her and held her in my arms crying and whispering in her ear all the stories she had told me of our family—going all the way back to when my grandparents had come to this country over a hundred years ago. I felt like a little girl again, hugging my mother for comfort, and feeling the warmth of that unconditional love she always gave me. Yet, I knew that soon, I would never be able to hug her again.

Both my father and my mother waited until I left their rooms—for one brief minute—to die, still protecting me to the end.

Chapter 13

People Want To Give Us Money

Dear Family and Friends: It is Fall, 2006, and as the mornings become brisk and the evenings turn cool for us desert dwellers, I realize that Fall is upon us. Time again to send my erudite words to you—whether you want them or not.

Rob and I have become very popular these past few months. I know this, because we get so many letters offering to give us money. In fact every few days some company sends us a faux credit card or neutral checks extending us an invitation to borrow up to $50,000 or $75,000 at 0% interest. We are already pre-qualified. How about that! Gosh, this makes me feel so good about myself. These people are ready to give us enormous amounts of money at no interest rate just because we're so special. I'm not telling any of our friends, because they may become envious of our good fortune.

Not only do we get offered loans, but an important looking envelope came the other day extending us $150,000 in life insurance with no medical exam needed—only a few yes or no questions—like, "Have you ever had any type of disease or surgery in your entire life?" If you answer yes, then you can still get the insurance, but if you die from any of these diseases or further surgeries, the policy is null and void.

I've decided to give my New Year's resolution an early start, so that by January, 2007, I will have accomplished my task. Since there are so many problems in the world that so overwhelm me, I've decided, "If not now, when? If not who, me." So, as a real challenge I'm going to lower my eyebrows! Some people have commented that I always look surprised because my eyebrows are so high. Well, something needs to done, and I'm the person to do it. I may have a "uni-brow" for awhile, so try not to gasp the next time you see me. Eventually, my brows will lower, and all will be well with the world.

Another feature of my anatomy that needs changing is my scalp. As I age my body seems to be growing these ugly bumps on my head. I have three now, and another starting to show its "head," so to speak. I've spoken to my skin doctor about these bumps. She said they are benign cysts, and that some people are cyst producers. I'm privileged enough to fall into the cyst producer category. Some people are just lucky, I guess. (I hope you aren't eating while you're reading this.) I asked her to remove the cysts, but she said, if she did, it would leave crater-like holes in my head. I said, "...better crater-like holes than becoming the Elephant Woman."

The rest of my letter was written by our cat, Ginger. She insisted on "equal time" since Gort wrote the summer letter. We try to avoid sibling jealousy.

My name is Gingie and I belong to Rob and Rita Davidson. I am a multi-colored, nine-year-old cat with sparkling green eyes that have a hint of amber in them. I've been told they are quite lovely. I take great pride in my appearance, and cleanliness is next to Godliness with me. I wash my face and paws after every meal, and I eat slowly, savoring my food. So you can see why living with a seventy-pound galoot of a dog with a penchant for giving off gas, drooling, snoring loudly, and eating as if each meal were his last, would be extremely irritating.

I am an indoor cat with all the privileges that go along with that. I was here way before this monster of a dog. I have the run of the house. I sleep where I want and when I want—without interruptions. I exercise daily by racing around the perimeter of each room. My intellect leads me into exploring strange and dark places to see what's inside. I prefer to examine paper bags and linen closets. But if these are not available, I might resort to freshly laundered underwear that my owner Rita sometimes places on the bed; unlike, Gort, the aforementioned ruffian of a bulldog, who likes to sniff the stinkiest of places—floor carpet and people's underwear—while they're still wearing it! One time, after one of his sniffing expeditions, he had the gall to come over to me and try to lick my face. Well, I showed him. I hissed and hit him over the head with my paw. I didn't hurt him, but it surprised him, and he backed off. I am a LADY! I will not tolerate any cleaning of the face except by me.

Once in awhile my curiosity does get me in trouble. Like the time I crawled into the dryer to explore the interior. The door swung shut. I thought I was a goner, but due to my superior intellect, I devised a way to get out. I cried and meowed and flung myself against the door of the dryer until my mistress heard me. She opened the door, just as I was pulling myself together, and I strutted out just as "cool" as you please. I meowed indignantly at her as a reprimand for her slowness. Next time she'll speed it up.

It's nap time for now. So live by my motto: Relax, relax, relax. Wishing you lots of gentle neck rubs, I Remain, Princess Ginger

Chapter 14

The Compromise

His given name, "Dollar," was a premonition of the future. But he was part of the compromise, and a deal is a deal. My husband, Rob, got his English bulldog and I got a larger house. A good marriage is after all about compromise, isn't it?

So that's how we got our English Bulldog, whom we renamed Gort, after the robot that came to earth with the alien in "The Day the Earth Stood Still." My husband is a big sci-fi fan.

Gort came into our already over-populated pet home to join two cats, Mousie and Ginger, and our German shepherd, Mattie. Immediately the animal hierarchy changed. Gort wanted to play with Mattie. Mattie was used to playing with Ginger. Mousie disregarded them all. Mattie sniffed this strange-looking creature and decided to ignore him. She did this for about three weeks. Then I made the mistake of starting to encourage Mattie to play with Gort. Finally I seduced Mattie into lunging at Gort while he rolled on the floor. Lots of barking and baiting ensued, and then I screamed for them to stop.

Now, my mornings consist of letting both dogs out, then feeding them (in separate, sealed off rooms, of course), and watching and listening to them bark and roll for what seems to be an eternity. Finally, Gort grabs one of his many chewies and begins crunching on it. All this activity exhausts him, thank heaven, and he conks out.

My husband loves this dog! Why? Because, according to Rob, he has character. Well, I can verify that he has gas and lots of it. He also has the thickest saliva I've ever wiped off the tile floor. His snoring can be heard throughout the house. If these characteristics bestow "character" then he does have a lot of it!.

Now comes his health record. Not too great for a dog who is only ten months old. So far he has had two eye surgeries to tack down a red membrane that pops out of his right eye. This condition is known in the highest of veterinarian circles as a "Cherry Eye." Unfortunately, the eye still looks the same—$1100 later. I've suggested we put a black patch over this eye to give Gort a dignified appearance. This might counterbalance his drooling and farting and give him even more "character."

On top of all this, he has had a "skin condition" for the last five months whose origin is still a mystery to the two vets to whom we've taken him. Tufts of his hair fall out causing bald spots. Of course, this makes Gort even more distinctive, thereby, giving him even more "character."

It has cost us $500 to run tests to see what he could be allergic to. Along with tests comes the fun of showering with him and shampooing him with special shampoo and then applying a cortisone ointment to his skin. He also gets an antihistamine pill in his food. With all this, his skin condition is getting worse. I have a feeling that Gort is allergic to us.

EXCHANGE *today*

Official Publication of the National Exchange Club
July/August 2007

National Convention/Symposium highlights

New National President Rob Davidson
   and First Lady Rita

50

Chapter 15

Gort 's publicity goes to his head. September, 2007

Dear Family and Friends: It has been three weeks since the Exchange Magazine has come out with our picture on the cover. We are so proud of the picture and Rob's interview. Now the responsibility of leading this distinguished community service organization has sunk in. We are full of hope and promise of a year of membership growth, community projects that make a positive difference in our cities, and the name Exchange becoming a "buzz" word for fellowship and compassion.

Of course, since the magazine has come out, we have been receiving calls from owners of fancy, female dogs who like the brawny, bold look of Gort. They want to know if we could "hook up," so to speak, Gort with their little princess. Unfortunately, we have to tell them that Gort has been "fixed." As they repeat this I sometimes hear a faint whine or a loud sigh from their end of the line. Again, Gort has broken many hearts. I can't imagine why these females find him so alluring. Maybe it's his large tongue that hangs out so seductively with promise. If they knew the places this tongue has been, they might not get so worked up. But, dogs like sniffing out the foulest of odors. I know Gort enjoys getting a whiff of road kill when we take him for a walk. A juicy bug now and then or a leafy twig makes for a bit of a snack between meals. However, if these feminine canines could observe Gort vacuuming up his meals or drooling over an incoming treat, I have a feeling they would move on to a "classier" dog like a sleek collie or a handsome golden retriever. And let's not get into the aromas emanating from his rear ALL DAY LONG. I'm talking frankfurter farts—not Estee Lauder White Linen.

Since Gort has seen his picture on the cover, he has been insufferable. His head has swelled to the size of a basketball and he has been strutting around the house demanding an agent so that he can do television commercials or more photo work. I told him that bulldogs are no longer in great demand since Zelda the Bulldog has flooded the market with her greeting cards and calendars. He claims his coloring is prettier than Zelda's and he's not as fat. I'll feed him a few of his favorite treats and then he'll lie down for a nap. His memory is short except when it comes to food, so if I hide the magazine, his fifteen minutes of fame will quickly be forgotten as he gobbles up his next meal.

Love and peace to you all, Rita, Rob, Gort, and Gingie

Chapter 16

Gort Goes to the Vet

You will have to excuse me for not writing sooner. These last three months have been very trying for me. Rob and Rita have been gone a good chunk of time. They are busy going to Exchange Club District Conventions back and forth across the United States. One week they are in Connecticut and New York and El Paso, the next week they are in Oklahoma, and last week they were in Atlanta. Our house sitter is okay, but she doesn't give me the constant treats I get from Rita. She cooks but not as much falls on the floor as when Rita cooks. I am starving!

The other day Rob takes me for a ride, which I really enjoy, because riding in the car gives me a "high." I jump from the front seat to the back seat to the front seat again. This way I can get a view of what's coming and what's going. Rob yells at me, "Sit down!" What's the fun in that! By the time we reach our destination I am very excited. There are so many great smells outside this place it's like perfume for my soul. Then I add my scent and pee. We enter the building. There is a scale I must stand on. It is really embarrassing when the lady behind the desk calls out my weight. I've gained seven pounds.

There is a good-looking greyhound over in the corner. I try rushing to her but Rob spoils all my fun by pulling me back. Some lady pokes her head out from behind a door and yells my name, "Gort Davidson." Now I realize. I've been here before. It's the vet's office.

We enter a smaller room. The vet and his assistant do the usual torturous routine on me—temperature, very uncomfortable; looking in my ears and mouth; and checking my heart and paws. I know to hold still because I see a large jar of treats on the counter above me. I have a good feeling that if I behave I'll get one. The vet says I have a thyroid problem. I am too sluggish. I need some pills. I hope they're liver-flavored!

I get in the car to go home and fall asleep. This ride and the vet's office is exhausting. When we get home, Rob tells Rita the vet said I was too sluggish and need some pills. "How could he tell?" says Rita sarcastically.

I agree. I am not the fastest dog on the block. I enjoy my "creature comforts." I live for food and long naps in cool places, a good Nylabone once in awhile, and a ride in the car—but not to the vet's.

Chapter 17

Dear Family and Friends: Today is my birthday. I am seven years old which I am told makes me a senior citizen. I've just received my AARD (American Association of Retired Dogs) card in the mail. From what I've heard, I am now entitled to all kinds of discounts and services befitting one of my wise years. The offers on the Internet are overwhelming: a complimentary colon cleanse. If this is anything close to the vet taking my temperature up my tushy, it's not for me. There are free ways to minimize bloating. (I know Rob and Rita would appreciate this, as they have sometimes had to run from the room when I give off a stinker.)

There are also offers for teeth whitening, but my Nylabone seems to do the trick for me. The other day I saw an ad for a green tea anti-wrinkle cream. As a bulldog, I don't worry about wrinkles—a few more here or there is no big deal. What else will they think of to do with green tea? My mistress, Rita, drinks a lot of it. I tried a few sips, but the only way I would ingest it is on a nice, juicy steak. Last, there are a lot of ads for lip plumpers. If I tried to plump up my lips, I don't think I could get my teeth into my mouth. Plus, I don't want anything that interferes with my eating. Eating is my biggest pleasure in life, though it doesn't last long enough as I am known to gobble my food down rather quickly. My advice for a long, healthy, happy dog life is to eat what you want (bugs are off limits, though); sleep a lot; chase the cat around the house once a day for a minute of brisk exercise; and round it off with a good belly rub from the suckers (I mean "people") who care for you. I am wearing a tee-shirt that says "All I got for my birthday was a bath!" Oh, well, I did get a large tablespoon of canned dog food, which I enjoyed immensely, to get me into the shower. My Master, Rob, sprayed some cologne on me for my birthday. Grandma, Clara, is coming over tonight to celebrate my birthday. I hope she brings me one of those great peanut butter organic treats. They're my favorite. Wet, slimy, kisses to you all. Gort

Chapter 18

From the Floor of Gort

Dear Family and Friends: It's been quite awhile since I took paw to keyboard to write you. I've been very busy the last few months what with eating, sleeping, pooping and peeing. My servants (no longer referred to as master and mistress) have renamed their house "Gort's Castle." They say I run the place, them included. I received my AARD card from the American Association of Retired Dogs a few months ago, as I turned seven, which in dog years, makes me a senior with all the privileges therein. Rob, one of my servants, says that actually I have been retired my whole life. Now I can demand discounts on my dog food and treats, vet appointments, and doggy toys.

The other day the cat, Ginger, who I am forced to live with, batted a fortune cookie wrapped in cellophane onto the floor. Well, with my advanced intelligence I scooped it up and chomped it down. Needless to say, her carelessness caused quite a problem for me. I couldn't sleep all night. I kept panting; and I threw up three times. Finally, I coughed up the cellophane, but Rita, my other servant, could not find the paper that the fortune was written on. The fortune, and a few pieces of pistachio nut shells I trolled for the day before, had caused distress to my intestines. My senior body just can't tolerate what I used to eat when I was a youngster.

As a result of all this, my servants, Rob and Rita, took me to the vet. By then I was getting better, but he had to take my temperature the yucky way. Then the vet gave me a pill to calm my innards. Boy, I was glad to get out of that place even though I got a treat from the vet at the end.

Now I am home and settled into my old routine of eating, sleeping, pooping and peeing.

Love to all my fans, Gort Davidson, English bulldog, owner of Rob and Rita Davidson. On the opposite page is a picture of me being retired.

Chapter 19

Horror House

Horror House: Family and Friends: I am writing this letter again at the request of my mistress, Rita. She just went through surgery and is a little too weak to write her Holiday Letter. Being the loyal dog I am, I said that I would be happy to do it for her. Of course, for this I get my choice of dog treats for the month of November.

She said this letter WAS going to be about her and Rob's adventures in traveling for the National Exchange Club, but life turned upside-down for them about two months ago when my mistress was diagnosed with ovarian cancer, which can come from ovaries whether you have them or not. This may sound like an oxymoron, but come journey through the Wonderful World of Medicine with us and by the time you finish reading this, nothing will make sense.

My mistress had her surgery and was able to "escape" from the House of Horrors, better known as a hospital, six days later. She was drugged, stuck, poked full of tubes, had little rest, and was generally humiliated by being treated as inhumanely as possible. My mistress tells me that in polite, people society, giving off gas and having a BM are not the usual topics of elegant dinner conversation, or for that matter even fast food dinner conversation. But, in hospitals, every worker who comes into your room asks, "Have you passed gas, today?" "Did you have a bowel movement, yet?" The incentive is that once you can do this you can go home. Rita said that she has never seen so many people concentrating on their bowels as she has in the Horror House. Patients would do anything to escape further torture, so they'd walk up and down the Horror House hallways trying to get their intestines working again. The first BM was celebration time, as going home was not far behind—so to speak.

Now that my mistress is home, we have some strange ladies coming to our house during the day. One lady, Rita says, looks like Aunt Bea from the "Andy Griffith" show. She cooks lunch for

Rita, does some washing, and likes to pet me a lot. I enjoy her, but Gingie, this annoying cat I am forced to live with, hissed at her.

It seems Aunt Bea has a couple of cats at home whose smell Gingie isn't fond of.

Rita wanted especially to tell all of you that every telephone call, every card, every flower arrangement, and every gift she has received during her illness has meant more to her than she can ever tell you. Right now I see tears rolling down her cheeks when she is telling me this. She told me that these are tears of love and gratitude to you all. You are all helping bring her and Rob through this tunnel on life's journey—once more to see the light. She says she loves you all and feels so fortunate to know so MANY wonderful people.

Gosh! Look at the time! It's almost time for me to pick out my first treat of the month for helping to write this letter. It's difficult to decide between peanut butter flavor or chicken, or beef, or pork. When you're a guy like me and just enjoy any food, making a decision like this one is tough. Knowing how I can wrap these "suckers," oops, my "Master and Mistress," around my paw, I have a good feeling that I can get one of each flavor today! Well, you ALL have a flavorful day. We'll be in touch. Love, Gort for Rob and Rita, and, I suppose, Gingie.

**An apology is sent to all English teachers or aficionados of the English language for all the dangling participles, split infinitives and misspelled words. Rita says that having cancer gives one some privileges. (better known as an excuse for poor grammar).

Chapter 20

Fun and Games with Chemotherapy:

Those of us who have gone through chemotherapy know how long and tedious the sessions can be. We just recline for four or five hours letting the chemicals drip into our bodies.

Exercise is recommended by some doctors while going through chemo. I have a few suggestions for exercising and having some fun, too. How about pole races? The patients line up on one side of the room holding their IV poles. An oncology nurse yells "Go!" Then the patients run to the other side of the room and back. Whoever gets back first wins a piece of candy.

Another fun thing to do is to start a betting pool among the patients to see who will finish their session first. (Whoever guesses the patient who completes their treatment first, wins two pieces of candy.) Beginning and ending times can be recorded by the nurses.

One great contest would be to see who has the longest scar. Patients' scars will be measured and recorded in private by the nurses. Players can put their answers on a piece of scrap tape. Whoever comes the closest wins three pieces of candy.

A real challenge is who can hold in their urine the longest before having to roll off to the bathroom. This may not be the best game for the nurses since it could get a bit messy. There will be four pieces of candy for the patient who wins, and five for the nurse who has to clean up the most puddles.

Last, one needs to let out aggression when a nurse can't access your port or arm vein. Instead of saying, "Oh, no, that's okay. It doesn't hurt much," scream at the top of your lungs, "They're killing me in here!"

Now who says you can't have fun in chemotherapy?

Chapter 21

The Wig

Having cancer is still very new to me. First of all, I never thought I would ever get cancer, since I took good care of myself—trying not to gorge too often and striving to exercise regularly. Three months after being diagnosed with ovarian cancer; being cut from stem to stern for the removal of a hideous tumor and two liters of yucky fluid, I now have two chemotherapy treatments behind me. As I run my left hand over the back of my head, my hair comes out very easily. I am losing my hair, which is no surprise, as many people told me this would happen. "Have it shorn immediately." "Let It fall out in clumps." "Shave your head completely." I got all kinds of advice, but yesterday I decided it was time to look for a wig.

There is a store in downtown Tucson whose window displays haven't been changed for at least thirty years, which put me off a bit, but when I walked into the store its walls were covered with hundreds of wigs—in all lengths, styles, and colors. Two small Asian ladies rushed up to help me. I mumbled something to one lady about going through chemotherapy and my hair beginning to fall out. Other than drag queens, I doubt if they see anyone else but cancer patients in this store.

As I walked through the store gazing at the myriad of wigs, I realized I hadn't worn anything resembling a wig since my 1967 purchase of an Oleg Cassini fall. Remember those? The comb piece locked into the top of your head and thickened your hair by twice. Of course, by the end of the day, I had a terrible headache from the fall pulling on my scalp.

The two little ladies scurried about the store picking out several wigs for me to try on. They ordered me to sit in front of this three-way-mirror, put what looked like a cut-off leg from a pair of pantyhose over my head, in case I had lice, and plopped a pale brown wig on top of it all.

"You looka vera nice," said one saleslady.

First of all, I didn't look "vera nice," and second, the color was not right for me. So I thanked them and began to wander around again by myself. "Here a curly one—real hair," the first shop lady said.

"Does it cost more than the synthetic hair?" I asked.

"No more," she replied.

Then I spied it. This was the wig for me. It was short, curly, and blonde. My real hair was short, curly, and black. I had to try it on. I looked like another person with this blonde wig on me.

"I'll take this one," I stated firmly.

The ladies sold me some shampoo and a stand shaped liked a woman's head to put the wig on.

I knew I'd get a lot of comments from family and friends, but I was ready. I wouldn't be the same person coming out of this experience with cancer as I was going in. The blonde wig was just an outward sign of the inner changes in me. Cancer can bring to our lives terrible suffering and fear. But it can also spark the willingness to try something new.

It is three years later. Much to my surprise, I am still here. My hair has grown back. I routinely have it dyed blonde. I am no longer the black-haired Rita of three years ago. I am the blond-haired Rita of today. I've faced death. I am not afraid. I live life one day at time and enjoy the hell out of being alive. Oh, I can say irrevocably that blondes definitely do have more fun.

Chapter 22

Dear Family and Friends: This holiday Rob and I decided do our shopping via catalog, since I haven't been able to get out much, and Rob has been so busy with me, his business, Exchange, and making sure his parents are cared for properly. We chose two catalogs with gifts we could not live without—Harriet Cartier and Walter Dreck.

I ordered Rob a T-shirt that says, "I Can Fix Anything! Where's the Duct Tape?" Rob is big on duct tape, and we still have a huge supply left over with large garbage bags from the scare of the millenium when all computers were supposed to go out. Hey! It's good to be prepared. I couldn't just give him a T-shirt without giving him some slippers to keep his feet warm, so I chose some sharp black slippers that say "Old Fart" in white letters on the top. What's so unique about them is they "break wind" as you walk. Being National President of Exchange requires some classy slippers that command respect. I think these "Old Fart" slippers are just the ticket.

Rob got me something I've only dreamed of: plastic toe flexors, They promise to give me "beautiful feet in just ten minutes a day." Gone are bunions, hammertoes, and calluses. He also got me some balls. Yes, between Rob and the steroids I take before my treatments, I now have balls. These balls are rubber, ribbed, non-toxic and fragrance free. They are dryer balls. I can toss them in my dryer to separate clothes so they dry with fewer wrinkles. What were you thinking?

Of course, we could not forget our two pests—better known as Gort, our dog, and Gingie, our cat. We ordered a book for Gort on HOW TO THINK LIKE A HORSE.. There's a section in it that teaches the reader how to speak like a horse. If we could get Gort to give up his snorting and to whinny like a horse, we could market him and get back some of the money we've poured into him over the years for his health problems. We also got him a

71

new drinking bowl shaped like a commode. Actually, it would be better to get him one shaped like a trough, since he drinks and eats like a pig. But, it wasn't available in that shape.

For Gingie, our cat, we ordered a musical walking turtle that moves its head and mouth and croons "You gotta slow down. You move too fast." Either she will chase it all over the house or freak out. Actually, we should buy her her own case of dental floss. She loves to take old dental floss out of the garbage and fling it around a room. Sometimes we find old pieces of dental floss in our bed covers. Always nice to cozy up in bed with some used dental floss.

Last, we wanted to get something for both of us. Traveling around visiting all the Exchange Club events and eating in hotels has caused us to put on a "few" pounds. Well, we found this wonderful weight-loss ring that helps you lose weight easily just by wearing it on a finger. Each finger you wear it on targets a different part of your body. Naturally, we ordered twenty—one for each of our fingers. This way we can be losing weight on all parts of our body at the same time.

Rob and I want to wish you all a Happy Hanukkah, a very Merry Christmas, a rewarding Kwanzaa and a healthy and joyous New Year.

Chapter 23

Dear Family and Friends:

You may notice that this year's letter is set in a larger font than last year's letter. This is for most of our family and friends who are in the "Baby Boomer" generation—sixty million of us now into our 60s. Hopefully, you won't need your bifocals or trifocals to read this letter.

Rob and I are now in the midst of our Exchange year as National President and First Lady traveling our beautiful country visiting Exchange clubs and Exchange fundraisers and Exchange conferences. We have met so many wonderful people doing

extraordinary acts of philanthropy in their communities. The Exchange club of Charleston, S.C. that raises over a million dollars at their Intercoastal Fair every year and gives most of this money to charities in the Charleston area; the Exchange Club of St. Petersburg, Florida that puts on a three-day rib fest netting over $500,000 which supports their child abuse prevention centers and is helping to fund the building of a needed pediatric hospital in St. Petersburg. Rob and I are overwhelmed with respect and admiration for these Exchangites who willingly give of their time and energy asking for little recognition other than the knowledge that they are doing good for their communities. In reality, they are performing miracles that affect thousands of families that they will never meet. That is why I want this holiday letter to honor all the Exchangites we've met and will meet in the coming year. They are our heroes, our knights in shining armor who've made the Exchange Covenant of Service a lifestyle. "Accepting the divine privilege of single and collective responsibility as life's noblest gift, I covenant with my fellow Exchangites: To consecrate my best energies to the uplifting of Social, Religious, Political and Business ideals: To discharge the debt I owe to those of high and low estate who have served and sacrificed that the heritage of American citizenship might be mine; To honor and respect law, to serve my fellowmen, and to uphold the ideals and institutions of my Country; To implant the life-giving, society-building spirit of Service and Comradeship in my social and business relationships; To serve in unity with those seeking better conditions, better understanding, and greater opportunities for all.

Have a peaceful and joyous holiday season and a healthy and happy New Year. Love, Rita

Chapter 24

HOLIDAY LETTER: 2008-2009—Dealing with telephone menus; Medicare; and Christmas Letters from People We Hardly Know

Dear Family and Friends: I am fighting for my existence to remain "simple," but technology sneaks into my life, forcing me to periodically enter the "Twilight Zone." Maybe you can relate? I called my doctor's office the other day and got this message: "Our menu has changed. Please listen carefully. Press one for new appointments. Press two for old appointments. Press three for a menu of office personnel by last name. Press four for referrals. Press five for a prescription. Press six to renew an old prescription. Press seven for directions to our new office. Press zero to speak to a real person. Press eight to redial this menu. Please do not call between the hours of noon and one thirty, as we are out-to-lunch. If you are experiencing a medical emergency (does this include a nervous breakdown?) dial 911 and an ambulance will pick you up and transport you to the nearest emergency room (an oxymoron), where you will wait six hours to be seen and another two or three to get a diagnosis. Whereupon, you may or may not be admitted to the hospital. If you're lucky, you won't be admitted, because bad things happen in hospitals like infections, rampant disease, and death. Have a nice day!" At the end of all of this, I forgot what I was calling about.

For the last month I have been receiving intimidating mail from supplemental insurance companies. It all started in November when a large book entitled MEDICARE 2009: WHAT YOU NEED TO KNOW came in the mail. As with many governmental manuals, I began trying to read "What I needed to know." I ended up not understanding "What I needed to know," so I had to call three governmental agencies plus the Pima Council on Aging to find out if they knew "What I needed to know." As far as I can deduce, as of this date I don't need to know anything. If I leave all this information alone, it will automatically be the same for me next year. So, this is "What I needed to know."

Who knew?

Rob is planning to purchase an extensive miniature racetrack which he wants to set up in our dining room on the 70" glass top dining table. I've convinced him the cars will look better on a folding table in the second bedroom. He has accepted this as a good plan. Thank God! Coming into this meticulously decorated house (okay, orange crates and bricks for bookcases aren't exactly part of the Ethan Allen line, but they are rustic) every day to look at a racetrack set up on the dining room table does not fill me with delight. Even our eclectic décor just doesn't lend itself to miniature cars, flags, raving fans, and peanut vendors. As an incentive for the dining room table idea, Rob promised I could have the fastest car. I can tell you, growing up as a little girl never in my wildest fantasies did I think I'd ever have a fast miniature race car! A few diamond rings, a real-size sports car, but never a miniature race car!

Every year for the last seven years we have received a Christmas letter from a couple we knew briefly as neighbors. Then they moved away. There are at least ten names of people (her family members? his family members? Santa Claus's extra elves?) whom we never met and don't know at all. It seems someone named Michael had to postpone his wedding plans to Barbara, and it's been hard for some kid named Steven to adjust to a new sibling. I'd like to help, but since I don't know these people I'll let a professional advice columnist like Dear Abby tackle these problems.

I'm going to forward their letter to her, tonight.

Rob's cousin and her family are coming from New York tomorrow to begin a six day visit with us. We've tried to plan an itinerary for them which will be fun, including trips to the Grand Canyon and Las Vegas. We are looking forward to having them—for six days. We have developed a sure-fire way to let guests know, though, when it is time to go home. We have Gort sleep in their bedroom the last night of their stay. The next morning, the results are evident. They are waiting by the front door, bags packed, ready to go as a result of lack of sleep from Gort's loud snores, and the dearth of fresh air from his frankfurter-like stinkers. I knew one day, we would find a use for Gort.

HAPPY HANUKKAH! MERRY CHRISTMAS! HAPPY NEW YEAR!
HAPPY KWANZAA!

LOVE, RITA AND ROB
GORTIE AND GINGIE

Chapter 25

Additions to Our Family

New Year's Letter, January 2010

Happy Holidays to everyone from the Davidson family. I am Ginger, AKA Gingie the cat. I am writing our family letter this year because I am really pissed and I need an outlet to express my feelings. My whole world has been turned upside down by my servants, Rob and Rita.

First of all, Gort, the bulldog, died at the end of October. Rob and Rita were so sad. They cried and cried. I, on the other hand, was so glad not to have the constant panting, snoring, slurping and gadawful stinkers to contend with anymore. The house was so peaceful. For a week and a half I was given the undivided attention I so richly deserve. Then Rob came up with this idea of getting on the Internet and contacting the Phoenix Bulldog Rescue. I was livid. He found two dogs waiting to be adopted—Lola, age seven, and Nana, age old. Rob sent in an application. Then a doggy social worker came to our house—my castle—to see if we were qualified to have these two dogs. She looked at the backyard to make sure there was no swimming pool or spa, as these two dummies don't know how to swim. They only know how to sink. Then she asked to look at Rob's and Rita's financial statement to make sure they could afford all the medical expenses these two canines will incur in the future. Unfortunately, they passed. These Bulldog Rescue people had found the suckers they were looking for.

Now I have two—you read it right—two panting, snoring, slurping, and stinky bulldogs to contend with. I think Rob and Rita can be classified certifiably insane. Not only are these dogs old, but one is deaf and blind, and the other is stone deaf. So who has to guard the house now? You guessed it—me, because they can't even hear the doorbell ring. Have you ever!

To add insult to injury, the dogs are allowed to sleep in the bedroom on special pillows. At night, Rob and Rita close the bedroom door, so I am relegated to the rest of the house, only because I jump on my servants all night long wanting to play. I am a night person—oops, I mean night cat. For Hanukah I am getting Rob and Rita this book I saw in the Harriet Cartier Catalog. It is called CAT TALK—WHAT YOUR CAT IS TRYING TO TELL YOU. It is supposed to teach them how to decipher my complicated personality and "understand my emotional and physical needs." I hope it works. Until then, you all have a healthy, less frustrating New Year.

Love, Gingie Davidson and Family: Rob and Rita Davidson, Lola and Nana Davidson (newcomers)

Chapter 26

A letter from Princess Ginger, cat of servants Rob and Rita Davidson.

Summer Letter—2010

This is a letter of protest. This coming week, because my servants, Rob and Rita Davidson, are going to the National Exchange Club convention, my castle is being invaded by two new humans, a huge, white dog with a tail that substitutes for a whip, and a new care giver for my Grandma Clara. Until now I have had to put up with a "special needs" dog (mostly deaf and really blind). This canine pants constantly, so her mouth is open all the time. What poor manners. Yet, the care giver for grandma just ignores me and gives the "special needs" dog treats left and right. Can this dog do tricks for treats?; Nada! She gets treats just for existing. I, on the other hand, get nothing for my humanitarian efforts. For instance, I have been investigating various piles of papers and paper bags that my servant Rita has been organizing to make sure they are properly filed. Sometimes, I turn the bag over and everything spills out. Why Rita gets upset with me, I don't know. This is a new challenge for her to get the papers back in order. I even help Rita exercise. Every morning I go around the house and tip over all the waste baskets. This gives her a chance to do her daily squats and stretching by picking up the debris and righting the waste baskets. Not only do I help maintain the physical health of my family, but I bring laughter to them by playing with used dental floss and riding on the seat of grandma's rolling walker. Do I get any treats for that? Not on my watch. I still do my morning exercise routine (a girl has to watch her figure) by racing through the house several times and then pawing a feather-filled basket (for muscle tone). These feathers are dust catchers. My pawing causes the feathers to wave, thus removing some of the dust. But do I get a thank you for that? Not a pat. One of my hobbies is to re-arrange silk flowers. My creations are more elegant than the originals, as I spread the flowers out so the colors and shapes are differentiated (Pretty highfalutin' word for a cat with a brain the size of a walnut). However, as you have probably perceived from my letter, I am no ordinary feline. I am "gifted." I like to read the newspaper. But, here again I run into flack because I read it while Rita is trying to read it. I like to lie on top of the paper while she is eating breakfast. This is something we can do together but Rita gets upset with me for it. I never win. To top it off, the "special needs" dog gets to sleep in the bedroom ALL NIGHT with my servants Rob and Rita, while I am relegated to the rest of the house just because I've been known to jump on Rob's "privates" in the middle of the night. I don't do this every night. Sometimes I jump on his face. Another complaint I've had is from Grandma Clara. She doesn't like it when I walk across the kitchen counters. She thinks it is unsanitary. The nerve! I clean myself every day, and probably am the most sanitary person in my castle. But Grandma Clara has never lived with animals before so she has a hard time appreciating my cleanliness. This coming week is going to be traumatic for me, so I may spend most of it under the bed where I can get some peace and quiet from the Neanderthals who are going to invade my domain. You all have a great time in Palm Springs. Yours in catnip, Gingie.

Chapter 27

Dear Family and Friends:

I'll just blurt this out. After thirty years of marriage, I've discovered that Rob is in love with another woman. Her name is Lola. She is around my age. At least he didn't pick a young bimbo. To add insult to injury, she lives in our house! Rob has been having an affair with her for a year right under my nose. Every night he comes home and the first name out of his mouth is "Lola. How's my baby, Lola been today?"

She runs up to him, and he gives her a huge hug. I used to be numero ono. Not anymore. How can I compete with her? She has too many things going for her. Her skin is smooth and silky. She is mostly blind and almost deaf, which illicits a lot of sympathy from Rob. Lola knows how to get attention. She comes up to your foot and places her foot on yours and rubs until you touch her. She needs a lot of help because of the medications she must have every day—ear drops, eye drops, three kinds of pills. Plus she needs her face cleaned and creamed every day.

She sleeps with us and her snoring sounds like a train locomotive going through the bedroom. The snoring doesn't keep Rob up at all, but I can't get to sleep for at least an hour. It seems strange to me that Lola's snoring doesn't budge Rob, but if I quietly get up to go to the bathroom during the night, Rob sits straight up in bed, "Wha, what's happening? Are you all right?" he yells.

Lola and I have some similarities which probably attracted Rob to her in the first place. We both could afford to lose a few pounds, and our bellies are rather large. These aspects of her figure just seem to make Rob love her all the more. He enjoys rubbing her belly and Lola is learning to love it, too.

As you've probably surmised by now, Lola is a dog in the literal sense of the word. She is our latest in a string of three bulldogs. We purchased her from the Phoenix Bulldog Rescue Club. She cost us three hundred and fifty dollars. That was in November, 2009. Since then, I'd say with all her medications, check-ups, and grooming, we could add another thousand to that. Mistresses, be they human, animal, or car, cost money. Oh well, as some great philosopher said on his death bed in the poor house, "It's only money."

Speaking of money, I received my pay stub for my pension yesterday. It's gone down another $100 a month. Where did the $100 go? You probably guessed already. My health insurance premium went up by—$100. Along with my pay stub, I received a notice from my Group Health Insurance Policy that all materials submitted to them now go to a new address: 185 Asylum Street. I kid you not. That is the address: Asylum Street. I think I've already been to that street a few years ago when some expert was trying to explain the three-hundred-page "booklet" on Medicare to me.

Before I close, I want to let all of you know that I am publishing a book containing twenty years of my writings. It should be out by the end of January. I am learning a lot about book publishing while driving a young lady at the publishing company to Asylum Street. My lack of computer knowledge has tried her patience on many occasions but she keeps smiling, and sighing, as she tries to correct all my computer errors. I will be calling her again tomorrow. It seems the last few stories I e-mailed her weren't in any order that she understood. I'm sure she is eagerly awaiting my call. I hope she had a restful holiday season because she will need every ounce of patience she has to deal with me.

HAPPY 2011 TO YOU ALL. LOVE, RITA

REGARDS TO ALL FROM HUBBY, ROB

MOTHER-IN-LAW, CLARA

LOLA, THE BULLDOG

GINGIE, THE CAT

note to printer – airbrush out lumpy neck – RJD.

RITA IRWIN-DAVIDSON is a retired educator who taught "crowd control" for thirty-seven years. She lives in Arizona with her husband, her mother-in-law, a dog, a cat and lots of cacti. She doesn't tweet and you can't find her on Facebook. She tries to maintain her sanity by living a simple life while commenting on the foibles of American society.

Made in the USA
San Bernardino, CA
05 September 2017